Tadpoles and Frogs

Carter Hayn

I0808441

Rosen REAL READERS

Rosen Classroom™
New York

Frog eggs are found in ponds.
Tadpoles grow inside the eggs.

Tadpoles hatch from the eggs.

A tadpole has a tail.

The tail helps it swim.

The tadpole eats and grows.
It grows two legs.

The tadpole grows bigger.
It grows two more legs.
The tadpole has four legs.

A tadpole's tail disappears.

The tadpole is now a frog.

Frogs have strong back legs.
They help a frog jump.
Frogs jump far.

Frogs have sticky toes.

They help a frog climb.

Frogs have a sticky tongue.
They use their sticky tongue
to catch bugs.

Adult frogs lay eggs.

Frogs lay many eggs.

Tadpoles hatch from the eggs.

Words to Know

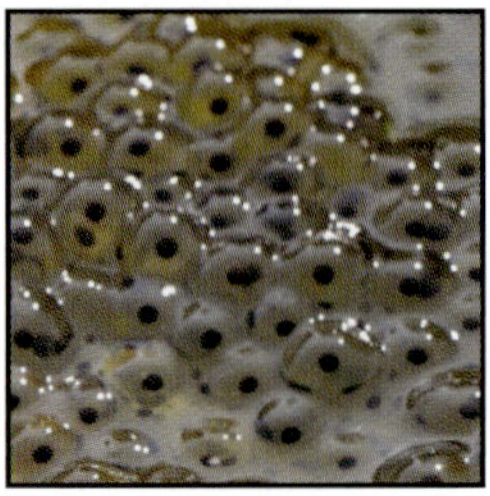

eggs

frog

jump

tadpole

toes

tongue